Vic   JUN 1 5 20··

ATOS Book Level: _____
AR Points: _____
Quiz #: _____ ☐ RP ☐ LS ☐ VP
Lexile: _____

I am growing and changing
Crezco y cambio

Bobbie Kalman
🌱 **Crabtree Publishing Company**
www.crabtreebooks.com

Created by Bobbie Kalman

Author and Editor-in-Chief
Bobbie Kalman

Educational consultants
Joan King
Reagan Miller
Elaine Hurst

Editors
Reagan Miller
Joan King
Kathy Middleton

Proofreader
Crystal Sikkens

Design
Bobbie Kalman
Katherine Berti

Photo research
Bobbie Kalman

Production coordinator
Katherine Berti

Prepress technician
Katherine Berti

Photographs by Shutterstock

Library and Archives Canada Cataloguing in Publication

Available at Library and Archives Canada

Library of Congress Cataloging-in-Publication Data

Available at Library of Congress

Crabtree Publishing Company

www.crabtreebooks.com   1-800-387-7650

Printed in China/082010/AP20100512

Published in Canada
Crabtree Publishing
616 Welland Ave.
St. Catharines, Ontario
L2M 5V6

Published in the United States
Crabtree Publishing
PMB 59051
350 Fifth Avenue, 59th Floor
New York, New York 10118

Published in the United Kingdom
Crabtree Publishing
Maritime House
Basin Road North, Hove
BN41 1WR

Published in Australia
Crabtree Publishing
386 Mt. Alexander Rd.
Ascot Vale (Melbourne)
VIC 3032

Words to know
Palabras que debo saber

baby teeth

dientes de leche

baby   baby crawling

bebé   bebé que gatea

toddler walking

niña pequeña que camina

riding a tricycle

pasear en triciclo

3

I am a baby. I was born today.

Soy un bebé. Nací hoy.

I am two days old.
I sleep a lot!

Tengo dos días de nacido.
¡Duermo mucho!

I am a baby.
I am three weeks old.
I have no teeth.

Soy un bebé.
Tengo tres semanas
de nacido.
No tengo
dientes.

I am four months old.
I can grab my feet and roll.
I am growing and changing.

Tengo cuatro meses.
Puedo agarrarme los pies y rodar.
Crezco y cambio.

I am eight months old.
I am **crawling** now.
I have **baby teeth**.

Tengo ocho meses.
Ahora **gateo**.
Tengo **dientes de leche**.

I am one year old.
I am walking now.
I am a **toddler**.
I am growing
and changing.

....

Tengo un año.
Ahora camino.
Soy una **niña
pequeña**.
Crezco y
cambio.

9

I am two years old.
I can play and talk.
I am growing
and changing.

....

Tengo dos años.
Puedo jugar
y hablar.
Crezco y
cambio.

I am four years old.
I am riding a **tricycle** now.
I can ride it fast!

Tengo cuatro años.
Ahora paseo
en **triciclo**.
¡Puedo ir muy
rápido!

I am five years old.
I go to school.
I am learning to read and write.

Tengo cinco anõs.
Voy a la escuela.
Aprendo a
leer y a
escribir.

I can do many things.
I can learn anything!
I am growing and changing.

Puedo hacer muchas cosas.
¡Puedo aprender
cualquier cosa!
Crezco y cambio.

All about you
When did you
start crawling?

Hablemos de ti
¿Cuándo empezaste
a gatear?

When did
you start
walking?

¿Cuándo empezaste
a caminar?

When did you start school?
Have you lost
your baby teeth yet?
How else are you changing?

¿Cuándo empezaste a ir a la escuela?
¿Se te han caído ya
los dientes de leche?
¿De qué otra manera
has cambiado?

Notes for adults

Everything changes

There are changes in the weather, the days of the week, months, years, and in people. Ask the children what changes have happened to them since they were born. What changes were there in their bodies—such as height, weight, color and length of hair, and when they got their first baby teeth and when they started losing them.

Have them create timelines for each year of their lives. Ask them to make a list of all the skills they have learned since they were born.

Baby you!

Invite each child to bring in a baby picture. Tell the children not to allow anyone else to see their pictures. Collect the photographs and post them on a bulletin board. Number each photo. On a sheet of paper, ask the children to write down the numbers and, beside each number, ask them to write the name of the student that they think is in the photo. After they are finished, reveal the names of the babies in the photos. Ask them how many of their matches were correct. This fun activity demonstrates that growth changes how children look.

Really big changes!

Show children a book about caterpillar to butterfly metamorphosis and ask them how their growth and changes are the same as, or different from, the growth of a butterfly. Can they grow into beautiful butterflies, too?

Notas para los adultos

Todo cambia

Hay cambios en el tiempo, los días de la semana, los meses, los años y las personas. Pregúnteles a los niños qué cambios les han sucedido desde que nacieron. Qué cambios hubo en sus cuerpos, tal como la estatura, el peso, el color y el largo del pelo, cuándo les salió el primer diente de leche y cuándo se les comenzaron a caer.

Pídales que creen líneas cronológicas para cada año de sus vidas. Pídales que hagan una lista de todas las destrezas que han aprendido desde que nacieron.

¡El bebé eres tú!

Pídale a cada niño que lleve una foto de cuando eran bebés. Diga a los niños que no le enseñen su fotografía a nadie. Reúna las fotografías y colóquelas sobre un tablero de anuncios. Enumere cada foto. Pida a los niños que escriban en una hoja de papel los números y al lado de cada número pídales que escriban el nombre del estudiante que piensan que está en la foto. Después de que terminen, revele los nombres de los bebés de las fotos. Pregúnteles cuántas coincidencias tuvieron. Esta divertida actividad demuestra que el crecimiento cambia la apariencia de un niño.

¡Cambios realmente grandes!

Muestre a los niños un libro sobre la metamorfosis de una oruga a mariposa y pregúnteles en qué se parecen y en qué se diferencian el crecimiento y los cambios de los niños al crecimiento de una mariposa. ¿Pueden también ellos llegar a convertirse en mariposas?